ALIVE

Crabs

by Ann Herriges

BELLWETHER MEDIA · MINNEAPOLIS, MN

BLASTOFF!
2
READERS

Note to Librarians, Teachers, and Parents:

Blastoff! Readers are carefully developed by literacy experts and combine standards-based content with developmentally appropriate text.

Level 1 provides the most support through repetition of high-frequency words, light text, predictable sentence patterns, and strong visual support.

Level 2 offers early readers a bit more challenge through varied simple sentences, increased text load, and less repetition of high-frequency words.

Level 3 advances early-fluent readers toward fluency through increased text and concept load, less reliance on visuals, longer sentences, and more literary language.

Whichever book is right for your reader, Blastoff! Readers are the perfect books to build confidence and encourage a love of reading that will last a lifetime!

This edition first published in 2007 by Bellwether Media.

No part of this publication may be reproduced in whole or in part without written permission of the publisher. For information regarding permission, write to Bellwether Media Inc., Attention: Permissions Department, Post Office Box 1C, Minnetonka, MN 55345-9998.

Library of Congress Cataloging-in-Publication Data
Herriges, Ann.
  Crabs / by Ann Herriges.
    p. cm. — (Blastoff! readers) (Oceans alive!)
Summary. "Simple text and supportive images introduce beginning readers to crabs. Intended for students in kindergarten through third grade."
  Includes bibliographical references and index.
  ISBN-10: 1-60014-016-5 (hardcover : alk. paper)
  ISBN-13: 978-1-60014-016-7 (hardcover : alk. paper)
  1. Crabs—Juvenile literature. I. Title. II. Series. III. Series: Herriges, Ann. Oceans alive!

  QL444.M33H48 2006
  595.3'86—dc22   2006009510

Text copyright © 2007 by Bellwether Media.
Printed in the United States of America.

Table of Contents

Crabs are ocean animals.
Some crabs live in the ocean.

Other crabs live near the
ocean on the shore.

A hard shell protects a crab's soft body. Crabs **molt** as they grow.

Crabs leave their old shells.
They grow new, bigger shells.

The new shell hardens on the crab's body.

Other crabs find empty shells to live in. They move when the shell does not fit anymore.

Crabs have eyes on **stalks**.

Some crabs can wave their eyes around to look in different directions at the same time.

claws

Crabs have 10 legs. The front legs have **claws**.

Some crabs have one claw
that is bigger than the other.

Crabs use their claws to gather food. Many crabs eat dead plants or animals.

Crabs also use their claws to dig nests in the sand.

Crabs even use their claws
to fight.

A crab's other legs are for walking. Did you know that crabs walk sideways?

17

Some crabs have back legs shaped like paddles. They help crabs swim.

Crabs can grow another leg
if they lose one.

Crabs hide when they are in danger. Some crabs tuck their legs inside their shells.

20

Other crabs blend into their
surroundings to stay safe.
Crabs are truly amazing!

Glossary

claw—a hard, curved nail at the end of an animal's leg

molt—to lose the outer covering of skin so that a new covering can grow

stalk—a thin part that connects one thing to another; a stalk connects a crab's eyes to its body.

surroundings—the area around something; crabs hide in their shells or wear plants to blend in with their surroundings.

To Learn More

AT THE LIBRARY
Douglas, Lloyd G. *Crab*. New York: Scholastic, 2005.

Galloway, Ruth. *Clumsy Crab*. Wilton, Conn.: Tiger Tales, 2005.

Kalan, Robert. *Moving Day*. New York: Greenwillow Books, 1996.

Knutson, Barbara. *Why the Crab Has No Head*. Minneapolis, Minn.: Carolrhoda Books, 1987.

Tate, Suzanne. *Crabby & Nabby: A Tale of Two Blue Crabs*. Nags Head, N.C.: Nags Head Art, 1988.

Tibbitts, Christiane Kump. *Seashells, Crabs, and Sea Stars*. Milwaukee, Wis.: Gareth Stevens, 1998.

ON THE WEB
Learning more about crabs is as easy as 1, 2, 3.

1. Go to www.factsurfer.com

2. Enter "crabs" into search box.

3. Click the "Surf" button and you will see a list of related web sites.

With factsurfer.com, finding more information is just a click away.

Index

The photographs in this book are reproduced through the courtesy of: davies & star/Getty Images, front cover; BE& W agencja fotograficzna Sp.z o.o./Alamy, p. 4; Martin Harvey/Getty Images, p. 5; ryan fardo, p. 6; Jeff Greenberg/Alamy, p. 7; Nancy Nehring, p. 8; Ben Philips, p. 9; Dragan Trifunovic, p. 10; Matt Tilghman, p. 11; Seth Resnick/Getty Images, pp. 12, 17; Kim Taylor & Jane Burton/Getty Images, p. 13; Georgette Douwma/Getty Images, p. 14; altrendo images/Getty Images, p. 15; Mark Harmel/Alamy, p. 16; Malcolm Schuyl/Alamy, pp. 18-19; Andre Seale/Alamy, p. 20; Brandon Cole/Getty Images, p. 21.